Bert Bielefeld – Sebastian El Khouli

Design Ideas

Bert Bielefeld – Sebastian El Khouli

Design Ideas

BIRKHÄUSER
BASEL

Contents

Foreword

Design is a process that is hard to systematize or typologize. Designs are the result of different approaches, influences and a trial-and-error process, especially when students are taking their first steps in the world of concept generation and design. They try something out and often discover that its potential is limited, yet their idea usually leads to new alternatives and interesting paths. This combination of inspiration and joy, of setbacks and frustration, sharpens their understanding of the design assignment, and a design finally takes shape. Even architects who have been working in the profession for a long time and have a great deal of knowledge experience the design process in this way.

Every design begins with a search for an idea or for an intuitive understanding of how an assignment should be solved. This design idea is the start of a long journey on which the designer defines the idea more precisely, modifies it, adds details and repeatedly rejects results. The current book, *Design Ideas,* is confined thematically to the start of this process, which influences and sets the direction of both the path and, often, the results. Its goal is not only to depict a variety of effective approaches and sources of inspiration, but also to show ways to unlock creativity. The contents are meant to encourage students to explore individual topics and concepts in greater depth. The focus has deliberately been shifted away from specific architectural styles and dogmatic principles. What is at issue here is a simple, yet complex, question: how do I come up with an initial idea?

Bert Bielefeld, Editor

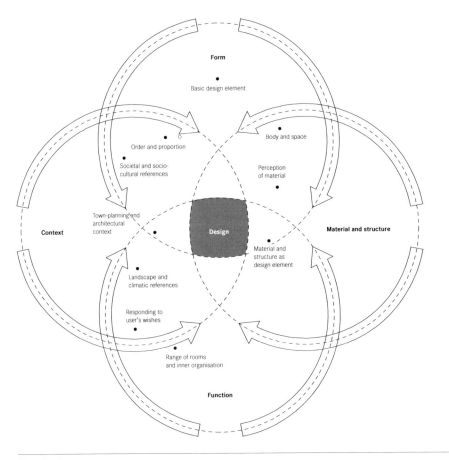

Fig. 1: Design map

Introduction

Architecture is not created in a vacuum. It is usually a response to the context in which it becomes constructed reality. Architecture is also expected to perform functions, to provide a concrete solution to an assignment, and to come to life through its design and materials. This is why the parameters set out in the "design map" – context, function, form, materials and structure – are directly related to every architectural design. > Fig. 1 They are also the elements in every design for a building. Furthermore, they hold the most potential when it comes to strategies for developing a design idea.

The following chapters will systematically present the parameters relevant to a design and analyze them with an eye to possible design approaches and concepts. Diverse links to other design-relevant factors will be mapped out to underscore possible points of contact and dependencies. These cross-references illustrate the way individual themes are intertwined and should keep you from getting caught in a dead end in the idea phase. In addition, the chapters will include references to exemplary buildings and more advanced texts on architecture so that you can carry out more detailed studies of the discussed methodologies and their architectural application.

These design parameters form a framework you can use when trying to generate your own ideas. They enable you to tap relevant sources of both information and inspiration in a structured way for your initial design steps. At the very start of the design process, it is often helpful to compile all the known information, conditions and perceptions and to visualize them in a consistent fashion. This exercise often reveals unnoticed connections and focuses, while pointing to existing gaps in knowledge and possible contradictions.

The final section of this book introduces different methods and exercises to help you take the first, and often difficult, "plunge" into the design process. It concentrates on the individual points of contact to your design work.

Design basics

The design process Design is a complex, often contradictory, non-linear process. This applies as much to the work of experienced architects as to that of novices, since it is the very nature of the beast. Even if the details of the assignment are clear, the goal of the process is unknown. Learning to design involves embarking on a quest for the methods that make it possible to recognize points of contact and dependencies and to understand the reference system of any given assignment. Architects then adapt these factors to architecture using their knowledge, experience, spatial imagination and creativity.

Every design poses new questions that give you the opportunity to gain fresh knowledge and to create a prototype tailored to the assignment. Designing is not only a central element that links everyone in the architectural profession. It is one of the most interesting aspects of the work.

Questions instead of answers When a new assignment begins, it is more important to ask the right questions than to embark on a hasty search for simple answers that might not do justice to the assignment's complexity. A large number of these questions will emerge from the immediate context of the assignment. An intense examination of the specific conditions of the design or of exemplary works of architecture can therefore be a promising way to approach the assignment. You can choose from a variety of strategies and methods.

Analysis and inspiration A common method involves the detailed study and analysis of the most important parameters:

— Urban planning context/landscape context
— History of the site
— User/utilization requirements
— Other buildings in similar contexts with similar functions

Linking this information with the results of analyzes will help you generate ideas that lead to a concrete design concept. In addition to doing scientific analyzes, you can pursue other, more playful methods that offer greater freedom because they entail fewer constraints. > Chapter Arriving at ideas

Another approach involves searching for inspiration or an idea at the very start of the process. The idea can be derived from the individual details of the assignment, its requirements, or even from sources of inspiration that bear no direct relation to the assignment. > Chapter Arriving at ideas, Methods and strategies As the work continues, other requirements and levels of design are gradually integrated into the concept. As a result, the design evolves in an ongoing transformation process.

The choice of the right method depends on a person's working style, skills and the concrete assignment. It can differ from design to design. All students should take advantage of the opportunity to try out different approaches and solutions in the course of their studies. The goal is to recognize the strengths and weakness of their individual approaches and to find out which approach suits them best.

Personal experiences and perceptions are decisive in the process of generating ideas. With every exercise, you will hone the tools of the design trade and develop a feel for the right path. Working with pens, a computer or a model is only a means to an end. The most important reward of constant practice is on an intellectual level. By leaving well-trodden paths, by trying out new ideas and designing by trial and error, you can tap into new veins of creativity and develop a diverse architectural repertoire. Developing creativity does not end with a university degree. It is a lifelong process that should be engaged in deliberately and intensely. Experiences

External influences not directly related to the assignment are also decisive factors in the design process. If the work on a design takes place in a team, ideas can emerge in dialogue with others, with each member of the team contributing to the process, advising others and finding the right path forward. The same holds true for an architect's interaction with a client, or with teachers evaluating assignments at the university. The exchange of ideas can help individuals grow beyond their limits, while the focused external feedback keeps them from throwing in the towel too soon and provides continued impetus. Students learn which methods do or do not help them achieve their objectives, and they benefit from the others' experience. > Chapter Arriving at ideas, Creativity and creativity techniques

Fig. 2: The appearance of a building is affected by its subsequent users as well as by the initial design.

Fig. 3: Local visits can show whether users have accepted the intended use of a building.

Spatial experience of architecture

Built architecture can also provide a wealth of experience. The intense study and physical experience of buildings is also a good way to become acquainted with ideas and methods. > Chapter Arriving at ideas While books introduce students to new worlds and serve as a source of inspiration during their studies, they are often quite selective and unable to present contexts in their totality. Students who take in a building with all their senses will have lasting memories and important experiences. It is essential to visit a building and experience it spatially, observing it from all sides in its surroundings. It is essential to touch and feel it, and see how people use it. > Fig. 2 This is the only way for them to get a comprehensive idea of the building and gain insight for their own work. Only if they experience a building themselves will it have a sustained effect on ■ their work. > Fig. 3

Developing a perspective on design

The experience you have with design assignments and your reflections on built architecture will gradually help you develop a perspective on how to tackle a design assignment. The term "design perspective" refers to a conscious approach to designing and to the way you adapt designs to constructed reality. This need not involve an eccentric, idiosyncratic style in the sense of a distinct architectural language. Rather, a design perspective is the unifying principle of a work and results from the way you deal with design assignments and projects.

This design perspective is often directly related to the designer's character, and is not limited to interaction with architecture. It can be

Fig. 4: Observing how a public square is frequented

Fig. 5: Light moods shift according to the time of day, and shade in a quiet area

an expression of an entirely personal worldview and associated with a broader social context or philosophy. Developing a design perspective is thus part of an individual maturation process and cannot be forced or artificially produced. When architectural students begin examining the architectural aesthetics and design perspectives of well-known architects, they are likely to look for role models and methods with which they can identify, and which they find adaptable to their work. They naturally find it helpful to understand the methods and perspectives already employed and to try them out or gain some experience with them in the designs they do at the university. This is the only way to explore recognized and famous worlds of design. But prospective architects should not shackle themselves to any single dogma that restricts their development and confines them to a certain path.

■ **Tip:** You should view as much built architecture as possible. A good way to start is by walking through your home city and carefully observing and analysing buildings on shopping or residential streets. This will give you a feel for the environment. It is equally important to study buildings designed by well-known architects. City tours, brief stops on trips, as well as excursions during or after your studies, all provide good opportunities to view the famous architecture in a region or city.

Designing in context

Each design emerges in a very specific context, whether it be a construction site and its surroundings, or a social and socio-cultural context.

While the process may begin with an examination of the site, the resulting building does not necessarily have to be adapted to surrounding conditions. An individual position or a counter-position can be formulated as an alternative. Even so, it is important to examine the site closely in order to understand the effects of certain decisions. Natural or anthropogenic influences will play a predominate role, depending on whether the site lies in a rural or urban environment.

Local presence   In most cases, the intense study of the site and its surroundings is extremely helpful in the search for a design idea. You should attempt to grasp the site three-dimensionally through sketches, measurements and visits, particularly if it has a distinct topography. You should also allow yourself enough time to study views of the surroundings and interaction
■ with the landscape.

Landscape models   If a broader landscape needs to be considered or the topography plays a particularly significant role, it might be helpful to build a landscape model that shows elevations. This can be used to check and optimize the effects that the initial designs have on the surrounding space. It is also important to study possible views on visits to the site and to select an appropriate section of the model. > Fig. 6 If larger contexts are to be portrayed – urban systems, views between buildings etc. – all important relations should be incorporated into the model. > Fig. 7 When preparing designs in an urban environment, you should also conduct spatial analyzes of the immediate and broader surroundings in order to get a feel for the location. These analyzes can take the form of as-built plans,

■ **Tip:** It can be advisable to visit the construction site and observe daily life at different times of the day. Where do pedestrians walk and from what perspective do they view the site? Where are quiet areas located, and where is there street noise? How are atmospheres created and how does the light change throughout the day (see Figs. 4 and 5)?

Fig. 6: Landscape model: architecture in a rural context

Fig. 7: Landscape model: architecture in an urban context

development structures, relations between streets and paths, the design of squares, green areas, and much more. > Fig. 8 In addition to the benefits mentioned above, the landscape model makes it possible to view the site from a distance on all sides and to discover connections that are often invisible from the site itself.

An examination of the location helps you understand the unwritten rules underlying the local situation. Systems, dependencies and relations between elements come into focus and cohere into a structure that can serve as a foundation for a design. The design can be harmoniously integrated into this structure or employ alternative approaches to interpreting it. Likewise, you can deliberately choose a "confrontation" with the surroundings or develop an autonomous design idea. It is essential that the work be based on an organic understanding of the place. If you ultimately seek a confrontation with the surroundings, this will be a conscious choice and should be comprehensible as such.

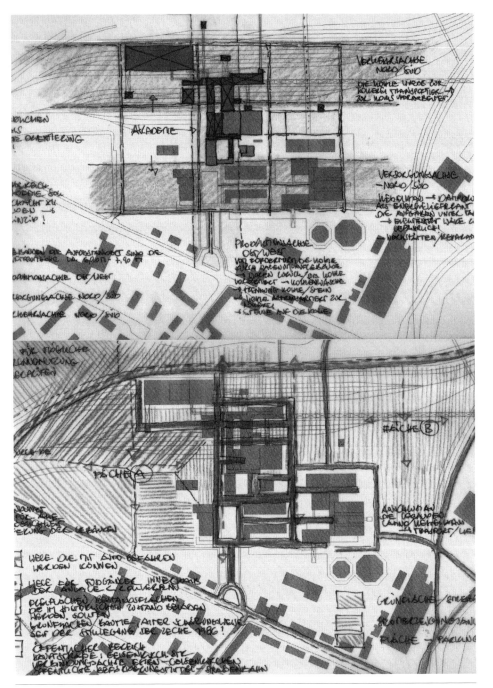

Site plans and on-site analyses reveal the unwritten rules of the location and help you develop design ideas from them.

Fig. 9: Sketches showing the effects of a lookout tower

LANDSCAPE AND CLIMATE

A study of the broader landscape extending beyond the individual site can yield a variety of strategies, from the design of a distinct landmark to efforts to simplify the visible, constructed building and adapt it to the surroundings.

Site typography determines how the design will be integrated into Topography the landscape. Regardless of whether the site is absolutely flat, sloped, terraced, tiered or hilly, topography will always affect the building and the subsequent interrelations between interior and exterior space. The type of terrain can also influence the layout of floors inside the building. > Fig. 10 For instance, height differences in the landscape can be continued inside the building, and entranceways can be positioned to use access routes to public street space. > Chapter Designing in context, Urban planning and architectural context Naturally, if parts of the design make it necessary, the site can also be landscaped. In general, a building can be designed to respond to the topography or even be playfully adapted to it. However, the architect can also make a conscious decision not to adopt such an approach and thereby create a self-contained unit that functions independently of the topography and establishes a clear separation between the surroundings and the architectural intervention.

When there are differences in elevation on a site of more than one Sloping sites storey, you must consider how the internal structure of the building is to respond to the topographical situation and what relationship should be established between the interior space and the surrounding area.

A building on a sloping plot can be set into the hill, project over the slope, respond to the slope with tiers, or modify the slope. > Fig. 11 These

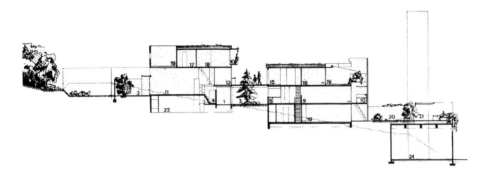

Fig. 10: Height differences within buildings

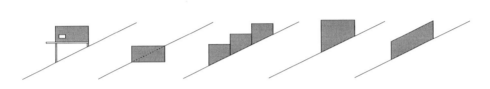

Fig. 11: Building types on slopes

different forms give rise to diverse relations between interior and exterior space. The special features of the topography, particularly on complex sites, often inspire intriguing design ideas. > Fig. 12 If there are broad views between the site and the surrounding landscape, you should determine both the angle from which the building will later be seen and the possible connections that might prove interesting in the landscape.

> Chapter Designing in context, Urban planning and architectural context

Climate-responsive architecture   Aside from site topography, an analysis of climatic conditions provides a further method for developing a design. Depending on the regional climate, it may be advisable to use the sun to determine the orientation and organization of a building. The building can be open on its sunny side, allowing solar energy to enter and be stored inside, or it can be closed off from the sun to keep heat out of the building.

Furthermore, the construction method, the materials and the architectural form can be adapted to the macro- and micro-climatic con-

Fig. 12: The view of the landscape as a basis for a design

ditions of the location. In warmer regions, buildings can be constructed as heavy structures or be set into the ground in order to use the storage capacity of the materials or the earth for cooling purposes. Alternatively, architects can facilitate cross-ventilation by exploiting the prevailing wind direction. In contrast, in moderate climate zones, the building's area/volume ratio can be optimized to minimize the loss of heat through transmission and to maximize the amount of sunlight falling on the facades. ■

URBAN PLANNING AND ARCHITECTURAL CONTEXT

In an anthropogenic environment – one constructed by human beings – human factors usually exert a greater influence on a design than natural ones. Anthropogenic factors can be analyzed in a detailed study of the environment with the goal of developing possible design approaches. The surrounding area usually includes neighboring buildings, streets or trees that form points of reference. There might also be additional buildings on the property that you will need to integrate into the design. If buildings abut the site, you will also need to clarify whether your building may (or must) be built directly alongside them. In densely developed areas where buildings stand on the edge of streets, you must also consider whether you want to adopt the form of the adjacent buildings.

■ Tip: More information on building to suit the climate in: Roberto Gonzalo and Karl Habermann: *Energy-Efficient Architecture*, Birkhäuser, Basel 2006.

Fig. 13: Building roofs influence the appearance of the urban environment

If the building fills a gap in a row, it might be necessary to respond to and interpret the different heights of the adjacent buildings. > Fig. 13 If the building stands as a solitary structure on the street, you can adapt the various existing systems or provide a counterpoint to them. Typical parameters in this type of analysis are:

— Roof type
— Building orientation
— Distance between the street and the buildings
— Materials
— Window type and size

Interaction with existing buildings   Most architectural assignments in the future will no longer center on creating new buildings on undeveloped tracts of land. Even now, there is a growing demand for ideas and plans of how to use existing buildings. Such assignments give you the chance to derive strategies that reflect the architectural distinction between the new and the old. You can put existing structures to new use, adapt them to suit modern needs, transform buildings, and give them entirely new identities. You can keep or add to developments (landmarked structures, flexibly used buildings etc.) or even individual building elements (facades, structure etc.). > Fig. 14 Alternatively, if remodelling and assigning new functions to existing buildings proves too costly, they can be completely demolished. In this process, an important question is the purpose of the architectural interventions: should old and new exist independently of each other as two distinct parts, or should they enter into an architectural dialogue? Should architects strive for extensive uniformity in a development or does quality a product of emphasizing differences? > Fig. 15 It is always crucial to ask whether demolition can be justified, or is even necessary, from an economic, environmental and cultural point of view. > Chapter Designing in context, Social and socio-cultural factors

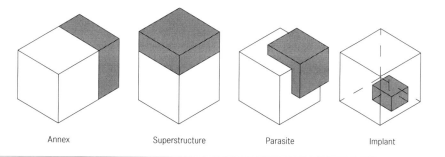

| Annex | Superstructure | Parasite | Implant |

Fig. 14: Possible extensions to existing buildings

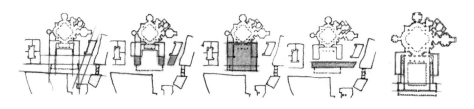

Fig. 15: A sketch analysing the use of the existing development structure

To avoid chaotic growth and the destruction of historically evolved structures, most countries issue detailed regulations on property development. These include:

Urban development parameters

— Restrictions or specifications concerning the building area or floor space
— Regulations on frontage lines and the boundaries within which a building can, or must, be built
— Number of floors
— Specifications on roof type and construction methods
— Regulations on entrances and circulation
— Distances to other buildings and property boundaries
— Protection of trees etc.

If you are designing a building that will in fact be constructed, these regulations must usually be observed. Furthermore, urban planning conditions need to be studied at an early stage of the project to ensure that the resulting design can indeed be built. Nonetheless, if regulations are strict and allow little freedom, there is a risk that familiarity with them will impede creativity in the design process. It is important to find a middle ground between the free generation of ideas and their implementability. This will determine the details you need to study and the depth to which you must go in your analyses.

Urban references and axes Densely developed urban environments often contain reference points and structures that, as overarching urban principles, have determined the design of most of the surrounding area. > Figs. 16 and 17 As part of an urban planning analysis, you should study the role and significance that your building's use or function will have in the broader urban structure and the immediate surroundings. You can also derive basic urban "figures" from this study as a point of departure for additional analyses.

For instance, if adjacent buildings are set back from the edge of the street, you can design a projecting building to create an urban accent. Alternatively, by designing buildings that are themselves recessed from the street, you can create a forecourt or a courtyard space. If the surrounding area already contains a number of dominant solutions whose axes and forms are incorporated into your design, the building will be well integrated into the surroundings and represent a subdued urban planning solution.

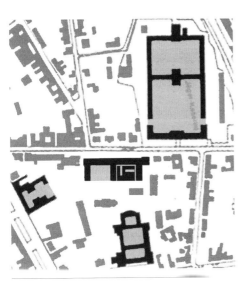

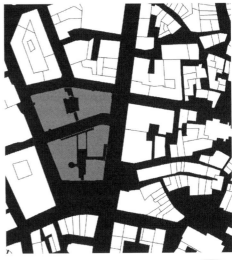

Fig. 16: Analyzing basic urban "figures" in a developed environment

Fig. 17: Analyzing how elements are integrated into an urban environment

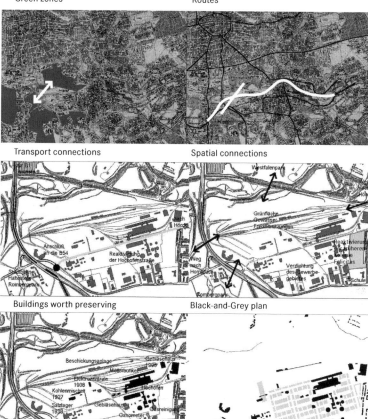

Green zones   Routes

Transport connections   Spatial connections

Buildings worth preserving   Black-and-Grey plan

Fig. 18: Analysis for the redevelopment of an industrial wasteland

■ **Tip:** In addition to studying local conditions, you can use area, city or land registry maps to conduct a variety of analyses (see Fig. 18). An as-built plan that shows the surrounding forms as blackened boxes will draw your attention to the urban building network and open spaces, while street maps will reveal important relations (see Fig. 19).

○ **Note:** For more information on the design and typology of public squares and spaces, we can recommend *City Planning According to Artistic Principles* by Camillo Sitte, Columbia University Press.

You will find further information on the urban-planning context in: Gerrit Schwalbach, *Basics Urban Analysis*, Birkhäuser, Basel 2009.

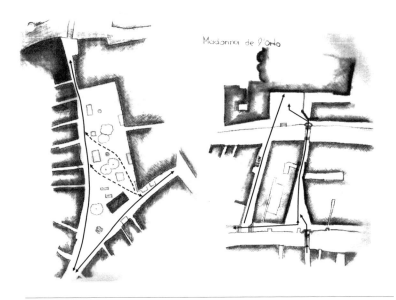

Fig. 19: Analysis of path relations on a city square

Depending on the surrounding area, important reference points or freestanding structures can provide a basis for dimensional relations and axes: an asymmetrical square creates edges with various angles, while an orthogonal street layout opposite the site opens up a view of the building. Alternatively, you can create a counterpart to an important element in urban space. There are diverse ways to communicate with urban surroundings through design.

○

Accessing the property and the building

Normally, you will already know where and how people access a property. The site either lies on a street, or has a path or road leading to it. Independent of functional requirements, access routes also determine they way users, visitors and passers-by perceive the building. > Fig. 20 An important question to consider is what effect the design will – or is supposed to – have on people approaching the building. > Chapter Designing in context, Social and socio-cultural factors

One important point is the height of the building's entrance level in relation to the street. If the entrance level is below street level, the pathway leading to it will seem to be of secondary importance. If the level is much higher, it is more likely to be perceived as "grand" and to inspire awe. If, on the other hand, a building is entered via a front square, the

24

Fig. 20: Access by means of a bridge, or via an axial staircase and portico

Fig. 21: The impact of diverse entrance situations

entranceway will create a sense of distance, even though it may appear more impressive. An entranceway through a courtyard divert attention from public space and create a commons area in front of the building. > Fig. 21 You should also consider placing the entrance to a building at ground level for wheelchair users, particularly for public buildings.

Building orientation is another point to consider along with the build- Orientation ing's three-dimensional shape, its position on the site and its entrance-way. A building can have a sealed-off and solid effect, or seem trans-parent and open on all sides. > Fig. 22 But these different possibilities lack orientation, that is, they will convey the same impression to all sides.

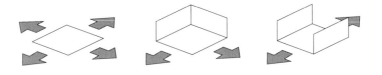

Fig. 22: Spatial orientation: open to all sides and not oriented; orientation to two adjoining sides; linear orientation to opposite sides

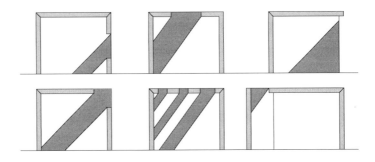

Fig. 23: Openings create different light moods as a result of their orientation to both the interior space and the sun (plan).

Depending on the site, you may want to treat the building's individual sides differently. You may, for example, desire to orient the building toward the sun, or need to design rooms with different lighting requirements. > Fig. 23 and Chapter Designing in context, Landscape and climate In moderate climate zones, orienting living space toward the sun is regarded as desirable, but it might prove disadvantageous in an artists' studio or a museum, since these spaces require uniform, diffuse northern light.

Other factors influencing a building's orientation can be found in the architectural environment. If the street side of the building is loud and lively, you may need to shield the residential and leisure spaces. The rear of the building may have an open park view that users would like to experience from inside the building. Or perhaps a large number of apartments are meant to benefit from a special feature of the landscape, such as a nearby waterway. > Fig. 24 These different situations may require a specific building orientation and inspire location-related approaches to developing the design. Examples include an entire wall of glass to emphasize a special view in an otherwise closed-off room, or perhaps a series of small windows that show specific details of the surroundings as an integrated composition. > Figs. 25 and 26

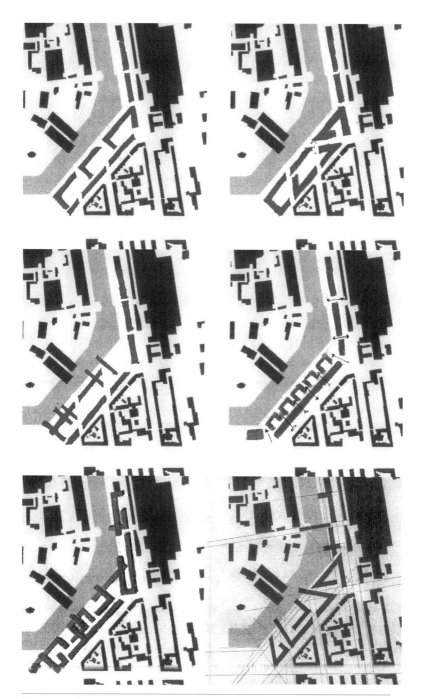

Fig. 24: Analyzing the orientation of a residential development on an inland harbor

Fig. 25: Orchestrated views of exterior space

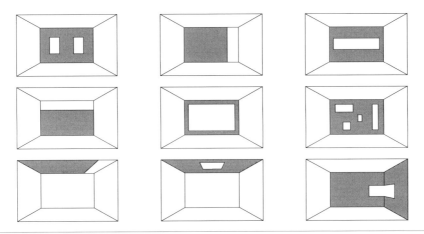

Fig. 26: The effects of windows: different orientations, orchestrations, communication and varying degrees of privacy

The relationship between interior and exterior space can lead to the development of a variety of architectural principles, from "closed/introverted" to "open/interactive." A glass house in a dense urban environment is probably ill advised due to its lack of privacy, but it may prove a good idea in a vast empty landscape where the building – as a minimal architectural intervention – will enter into a dialogue with the surrounding area.

If the building is meant to relate to its surroundings, the way it does so can be based on the external perception of the building or on the interaction between interior and exterior space. For instance, a panoramic window can be used to emphasize a lovely view of a valley, or a carefully

Fig. 27: Integrating the exterior space into a church space and its use

Fig. 28: Glass surfaces can emphasize interaction (through transparency) or convey a sealed-off quality (through reflection).

positioned window can transform an interesting visual axis into an effective element in the building's interior. A building can also be built around a prominent tree, which will then become part of the interior space. > Chapter Designing in context, Landscape and climate

Interaction between buildings and their surroundings

The use of wall-to-ceiling windows or specific views into and out of the building in order to differentiate open and closed spaces is an important design tool for creating a range of spatial experiences. > Figs. 27, 28 and Chapter Design and function, Responding to user needs

Differing elevations and views across the inside of a building can also play an important role in creating concepts. If outside areas are not shielded from views, the ensuing lack of privacy quickly diminishes their appeal. However, an interesting view from a shielded area can dramatically alter spatial impressions. The same is true of designs that optically conceal the boundary between interior and exterior space as a means of integrating the private exterior space into the building. > Figs. 29 and 30

For this reason, a building should never be considered only in isolation. If possible, you should examine the interaction between the property, the building and its use. A design is influenced by many location-related elements, such as shadows from adjacent buildings, sunlight at different times of the day (and during different seasons), as well as the provision or hindrance of specific views into and out of the building. These different aspects also show that a design always emerges from the interplay between the location and the diverse architectural requirements.

Fig. 29: Interior space with a fluid transition to exterior space

Fig. 30: Shielded exterior space with a view

SOCIAL AND SOCIO-CULTURAL FACTORS

The previous chapters addressed many factors that influence how people perceive architecture. In this connection, it is important to distinguish between the way architecture is perceived by the senses and the way these impressions are processed in the human brain. Even if sensory perception always remains the same, information is processed in different ways due to the differing individual thought patterns, which are, in turn, strongly influenced by personal experiences and social and cultural contexts. This explains why people will perceive an event or a building in different ways. Generally speaking, perception is not objectifiable, even if an "objectified subjectivity" emerges from the combined opinions of the great majority. This subjectivity is mostly confined to a narrow social, historical and cultural framework, since people are largely socialized and influenced by their education. An examination of the historical, social and cultural backgrounds of an assignment often yields important insights and can provide a source of inspiration for generating ideas.

The study of a location should not be limited to an examination of the immediate environment. Every architectural project is a response to the history of a place and plans its future. Designing and modifying an existing situation is an intervention that is inevitably perceived by those in the environment as a part of a continual process. Buildings are constructed and used for specific purposes. They can then be used in new ways, remodelled, added to, torn down, rebuilt or recycled. At times they may remain vacant or fall into disrepair. > Fig. 31 Their use often has a social significance, regardless of whether it is embedded in a broader history that is later recorded in books or in the more personal stories that people associate with specific places. Efforts to create references to the history of a place can lead to various approaches to developing design ideas. You can refer to collective memories – impressions made on the memory of an entire society – or to the entirely personal stories of the client or the previous users of the property. > Fig. 32 Similarly, you can gain personal access to a subject matter by incorporating your own experiences into the initial idea.

Historical factors

It is important to ensure that the reference system reflects the significance of the architectural assignment. For example, if the assignment has social implications – such as a design for a museum or a memorial site – it may be advisable and even necessary to focus on the link to historical events. But when the object of the design is a residential building or a shopping center, you should give careful thought to whether a historical reference is appropriate to the context.

Fig. 31: The addition of a glass hall creates a new use for an old castle ruin.

Fig. 32: Urban dialogue between a new cultural institution and a Roman temple

Fig. 33: Residents using public and common areas

The socio-cultural context

If your design idea is a response to social developments, you can derive basic approaches from either an overarching social context or specific phenomena. For instance, when conceptualizing a residential complex, you can attempt to counteract the increased privatization of public space by creating public pathways leading across the site or by integrating public facilities. > Fig. 33 Further, barrier-free accessibility to all parts of a building can have an impact on both urban development and access to the building.

One interesting aspect of socio-cultural analysis is that it gives you the chance to express your own views and philosophy: what mix of uses is necessary to integrate elderly people or those of different ethnic backgrounds into society? How much community and how much individuality are possible, and necessary, in our shared lives? What role does environmental and climate protection play, and how can its importance be

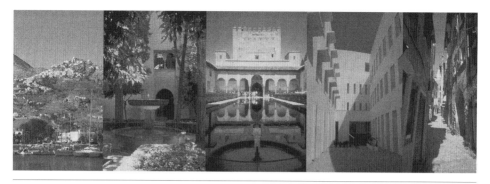

Fig. 34: Regional architecture in Mediterranean cultures

reflected in the design concept? What limits are there on development density if we wish to avoid mutually adverse effects and prevent the uncontrolled development of the landscape from worsening?

Whatever approach you choose, it is crucial that you relate the initial architectural measures to a broader context and value system. This will help you develop your own perspective.

Over the course of time, diverse regional architectural forms and typologies have evolved from different climatic, cultural and social conditions, as well as from the often limited availability of materials and from specific uses or utilitarian forms. > Fig. 34 and Chapter Designing in context, Landscape and climate

Regional architecture

Often, these architectural typologies offer astonishingly simple solutions to a variety of needs. Examining and analysing regional architecture can frequently lead to surprising new insights on the complex interrelations between architecture and architectural and social contexts. It is important not to view architecture in isolation from its function, its surroundings, and the period in which it was built.

In general, we cannot compare modern conditions to those under which many traditional architectural forms evolved. We have many more possibilities and materials for coping with challenges, even those involving difficult climatic conditions. Uses and requirements have also changed dramatically. As a result of the ongoing internationalization processes, the differences between places and cities seem less pronounced today than in the past. Materials and architectural forms have not only become increasingly similar, but our habits and behaviour have also become more and more alike due to our knowledge of other countries and cultures.

Internationalization

To develop sustainable architecture that enters into a lively dialogue with its surroundings, you should become acquainted with and respond to differences in regional and local architecture. Traditional architectural forms and typologies play a major role in this process since they strongly influence the way a new building is seen in its environment. For example, because of local architectural traditions, a new brick structure erected in the north of Germany or in the Netherlands will fit in seamlessly with the surroundings and have the appearance of a traditional building. Yet the same structure will stick out like a sore thumb in a town in the south of Italy where the buildings have monochrome rendered facades. The different moods of light in the Mediterranean region – marked by rich contrasts and warmth – make simple structures with three-dimensionally shaped facades appear much more dynamic than similar buildings in, say, Moscow, where there is a low-contrast light environment. Modern architectural forms are not randomly interchangeable or reproducible, and they are more closely intertwined with a place than they may seem at first glance.

Symbolism and iconography Architecture imparts information. This information can be perfectly obvious and recognizable to everyone, or it can hidden from view and only gradually reveal itself to the observer. In all periods of architectural history, people have discussed how architecture needs to convey information and how this information is related to the purpose and use of a building.

Two opposing positions can be made out: one school strives for a unity of content and form, following the principle of structural honesty. The other emphasizes the role played by architecture in carrying meaning and creating identity, independent of its purpose and functionality. This school uses the symbolism and iconography of individual architectural motifs to do justice to this idea.

In eclecticism and postmodernism, architectural references and motifs are used to trigger associations in viewers and achieve specific effects. For example, a building may appear more impressive if it incorporates the formal vocabulary of the Greek temple or the icons of modern architecture. The design will then allow viewers to draw conclusions about the building's purpose, function and owner. It is unimportant whether these assumptions are true or not. Outer shell and function are not supposed to form a creative whole. Rather, the architects who design in this way strive to separate the outer shell and give it a measure of independence so as to emphasize its role as a bearer of meaning.

○ ■ > Figs. 35 and 36

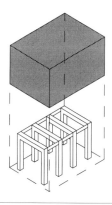

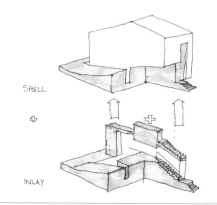

Fig. 35: The principle of separating a structure from its shell

Fig. 36: A residential building showing the principle of separating a shell from its structure

At the same time, architects can also make symbolic references to thematic parallels over and above formal references. For instance, during the Renaissance, there was a return to the values and view of mankind that prevailed during antiquity. In architecture and art, this was expressed in new interpretations of the buildings, principles and themes of antiquity. Nonetheless, it must be noted that a message that appears logical from a personal or professional perspective may be interpreted in an entirely different way by others. This is why you must analyze the cultural and social context before using stylistic devices such as symbolism and iconography. > Chapter Constituents of design

The relationship and interaction between architecture and other artistic disciplines can best be understood by examining the various periods of art and architectural history, remembering that art and architecture do not always apply the same principles and methods in any given period. One of the most important differences is that, aside from its

Links to other disciplines

○ **Note:** Symbols carry meaning, and their value lies in the way they unify content, meaning and form. Symbols represent an object while preserving its outer and inner unity. By contrast, when architects "cite" certain motifs, they do not aim for a unity of content and form.

■ **Tip:** Architectural symbolism is an extremely exciting and complex topic. For a more in-depth study, we recommend *Learning from Las Vegas* by Robert Venturi and Denise Scott Brown, MIT Press, 1977.

artistic ambitions, architecture must satisfy the elementary need that all people have for a place to live, work and sleep, and for protection from the weather. Even if these special functions give architecture a special status in relation to the other arts, there exist connections with these

○   other disciplines that can serve as a basis for producing new design ideas:

The periods in which art and architecture were closely related show most clearly which principles can be transferred from one field to the next. In the Renaissance there were significant parallels between the articulation of foreshortened space in paintings and the selection of perspectives in constructed reality. The goal of the Bauhaus was to combine architecture – as a synthesis of the arts – with all the other artistic disciplines to unify all the arts. The formative themes of postmodernism, including iconography and identification, are most clearly legible in its architecture. Numerous parallels also exist in contemporary art.

●   In their spatial and physical effects, outdoor sculptures display many parallels to architecture. The interesting interactions between an object and its surroundings can be used to train spatial perceptions. The parallels are particularly striking if the artworks have been created for a specific place.

○ **Note:** The arts are generally divided into four different categories:

The visual arts, which include painting, sculpture, architecture and the applied arts

The performing arts, whose main disciplines are acting (theatre, film) and dance

Music, broadly divided into vocal and instrumental music

Literature, which is subdivided into narrative prose, drama and poetry

Works of visual art are usually spatial, physical objects that have an effect in and of themselves and do not require an interpreter.

● **Example:** In his accessible spatial sculptures made of corroded steel plates, Richard Serra explores the nature of the material by showing its aging process. He also emphasizes its heaviness, with many of the sculptures weighing upward of 100 tonnes (Fig. 37). The powerful spatial and atmospheric effects of these sculptures are reflected in the unease that they initially caused in public space. Peter Eisenman, among others, has taken a comparable approach in architecture, particularly in his design for the Holocaust Memorial in Berlin (Fig. 38).

Fig. 37: Sculptures by Richard Serra

Fig. 38: Memorial to the Murdered Jews of Europe by Peter Eisenman

Even so, most works of art cannot be understood through observation alone. It is also important to read texts by artists, as well as secondary literature and biographies. Most artists have written extensively about their working methods and their motivation. It can be very rewarding to experience and try out work and design methods from the other artistic disciplines. By examining the various techniques of painting, sculpture, photography, music and other art forms, you can find inspiration for your own architectural work.

Design and function

The function of a building will usually have a formative effect on both its design and the way the design is developed. Depending on the your approach, function can provide a general framework that you must adhere to, or form a point of departure for design ideas. Many architects develop their buildings by designing a floor plan or spatial framework to fulfil certain requirements and functions. Drawing on their creative skills and experience, they derive from this a specific expressive style and formal vocabulary that transcends mere functionality and aims for a unity of form and function.

Function as the point of departure for a design Ever since the modern period, it has been common to use function as the basis for designs, and function has also assumed special importance in architectural studies. Creating a design that reflects and visually expresses function is a fundamental architectural objective.

The steps described in the sections below are offered as tools and possible approaches to help students understand function and to incorporate it into their designs. In principle, these steps are not required to create a "functioning" design, yet it is advisable to use such tools, particularly when the function in question is not one with which you are acquainted in detail. The term "tool" already emphasizes that these aids are not at the center of design work. Illustrating mutual dependencies in a functional diagram presupposes that you already fully grasp their intricacies. One way to understand them is to read publications that provide information on typical spatial needs or functional connections. > Appendix, Literature In addition, you can analyze existing buildings with identical or similar uses. Studying the plans of several exemplary buildings will show similarities and common rules as regards the layout, size and structure of the individual areas. These can be incorporated into your design.

RESPONDING TO USER NEEDS

When turning your attention to a building's function, you usually also have to deal with the people who need it, whether in the form of housing, workspace or recreation. It is important to analyze how users practise this function within the building, or how they wish to experience it. If we consider a cinema, for example, we can see that people expect a specific world of experience from this structure. They want to be entertained and perhaps even immersed in another world for a short time so that they can forget their everyday lives. Your design can take these expectations into account. By contrast, you should design an office workplace in such a way that employees can concentrate and are not interrupted during their work. You need to meet their expectations about lighting, ventilation, acoustics and workplace design.

There are different ways to study user needs: on the one hand, you may be personally acquainted with the user and thus know the person for whom you are designing the building. On the other, the design assignment may be focused on a specific target group (e.g. senior citizens who live in planned apartments) as opposed to an actual person.

If the user is known, you can study his or her individual interests and needs. For instance, if the assignment is to build a home and a studio for an artist, discussions with the artist and observations of his or her working methods can yield insights into requirements and needs. Perhaps the artist wants a quiet, uniformly lit and shielded studio space, or enjoys the view of the landscape or the hustle and bustle of the big city. Individual needs

You will face an entirely different situation when designing a structure for a specific target group. In this case, you must first get an idea of the group's general requirements. Here, it may be helpful to study local solutions and buildings in order to learn more about the target group's needs, or to analyze existing problems that exemplary projects with the same function have confronted. These problems can then be addressed in the design. > Chapter Arriving at ideas Focusing on a target group

In most cases, you can examine user needs by contacting them directly and sharing ideas with many different types of users. You should resist the temptation of attempting to understand internal processes (e.g. at specific production sites or a fire station) from the "outside" only. This is particularly important with functions of which you have little knowledge. The people who deal directly with a building's function on a daily basis will have a different view of things, and it is important to consider their views when you work together to adapt functional processes to spatial designs. The intense exchange of ideas with employees or users on all levels of an organization will help you analyze processes, structures and, most of all, problems arising in existing buildings. Even so, information obtained solely from users is of limited use in a design because they lack an architects' background knowledge of design. This is why working together on utilization concepts and detailed planning is the ideal way to design a building that functions well down to the last detail. Contact with users

SPATIAL ALLOCATION PLAN AND INTERNAL ORGANIZATION

Spatial requirements are usually given for definite construction projects. For instance, a family will have a specific idea of the house they want to have designed, a company will need workspaces for a given number of employees, or a museum will require exhibition space for specific exhibits. The necessary spaces and volumes can be derived from these needs and can provide an initial idea of a project's size and dimensions.

Space and volume

For standardized uses such as apartments and offices, you can arrive at a rough estimate of building volume by adding the space of the building's structure and secondary rooms, expressed in percent, to the required floor space and multiplying the result by a standard ceiling
● height.

Structures such as indoor swimming pools, museums and event halls usually include a variety of rooms, some of which have entirely different requirements for space and room height. This is why it is important to look at each area separately in order to address specific needs, and to design special features in the creative process. An indoor swimming pool might be a dominant structure in an ensemble of buildings, so that its subordinate functions can either be included in that structure or in other separate facilities.

If you decide to design in this manner, it is important you do not view the rough attempts at creating a structure as the actual design. Otherwise you run the risk of accepting the rough form as a given and not exploring the design in any greater depth. You should always keep in mind that the structure is an abstract figure and its form can be further modified as desired. > Fig. 39

● **Example:** Say a family needs about 120 m² of living space. To compute the total amount of space, add 20 to 25 percent for the space taken up by walls and shafts. Multiplying the total space by a floor height of 3 m yields a volume of approximately 450 m³. If you are designing a two-storey cubic building, this translates into an 8 × 8 × 8 m cube. Mental exercises like these can give you a sense of building size.

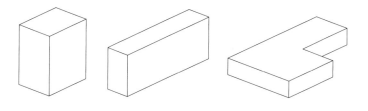

Fig. 39: The same volume as a compact tower, a bar and a flat, L-shaped building with courtyard

Tab. 1: Example of a spatial allocation plan

Consulting center

Function	Room size [m²]	Number	Total space [m²]
Reception area / assistants	40	1	40
Waiting room	40	1	40
Assistants	12	2	24
Director	40	1	40
Office	20	1	20
Group manager	25	2	50
Consulting room	25	17	425
Conference	30	1	30
Staff room	20	1	20
Toilets	40	1	40
Secondary sales area		15%	109
Total		**28**	**838**

In addition to making rough estimates of space and volume, it is important to create a spatial allocation plan that not only specifies the individual functions or rooms and their spatial requirements, but also divides rooms into thematically related groups. > Tab. 1

Spatial allocation plan

For many design assignments, the spatial allocation plan is already provided. Even so, the design assignment may sometimes involve developing the appropriate function together with the spatial allocation plan. Practising architects, in particular, often encounter clients who have a clear idea of the primary function of the building, but do not know what additional spaces and secondary functions are needed.

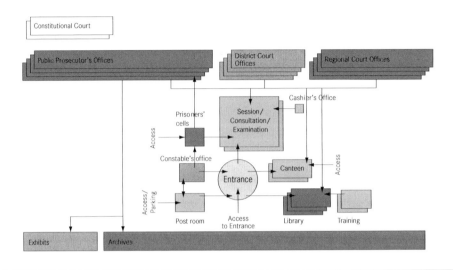

Fig. 40: Example of a scale organizational chart

Therefore, your first job is to determine the main areas of use as well as the required secondary areas such as the lobby, toilets, entrances and hallways. You also need to figure out the spatial needs of each area if you want to gain an overview of the entire design assignment.

If, for instance, a company wants to create office space for 500 employees, you must first determine the office type (individual offices, open-plan offices) required for the employees as well as the amount of space each one needs. The secondary functions and access routes must also be taken into account to get an overall impression of spatial needs.

You can take a similar approach to, say, designing housing for elderly people. Together with the client, you must initially determine whether individual housing functions need to be integrated into the residential units, or whether they should be organized centrally for all the occupants.

○ **Note:** For more information on housing functions, please see *Basics Design and Living* by Jan Krebs, Birkhäuser, Basel 2007.

The spatial allocation plan makes it possible to form groups of functions or spaces that have the same requirements as regards room height, lighting etc. It indicates the proportionate arrangement of spaces and will give you a feel for the size and proportions of the design. ■

To assess the design further, you can develop circulation and path systems that structure the building and provide information on its volume and shape. For example, if an office building consists of individual offices, you can examine how far natural light falls into the building as a way of determining the building's depth. This can then serve as the basis for designing the building structure. ●

Interior circulation and lighting

It can also be helpful to give some thought to the functional organization of the assignment. This should be expressed visually in order to determine the functional links between the building's various rooms and areas. One common tool is a functional diagram that graphically depicts all the functional areas or rooms and shows their interrelations. > Fig. 41

Internal organization

The diagram visually represents the building's internal organization. It reveals areas and connections that may have a formative effect on the design. For instance, if a private or sensitive functional area has to be separated from public or semi-public spaces, the resulting spatial layout may strongly influence the design.

■ **Tip:** At times it may be helpful to draw the rooms in the spatial allocation plan as true-to-scale spaces in different proportions. This will give you a visual sense of the arrangement of spaces in the design assignment.

● **Example:** Say an office building is a double-loaded structure with a middle corridor and a ceiling height of about 3 m. The maximum depth of the building can be determined by examining the maximum depth that an office can have and still be illuminated by natural light (approx. 5.5 m) falling through floor-to-ceiling windows. If you add the width of the central corridor (about 1.00 m), the thickness of the exterior walls (about 40 cm) and the corridor partition walls (each 15 cm), you will have a building depth of about 14 m. If the offices are arranged as combi-office zones, you can create a building depth of up to 16 m.

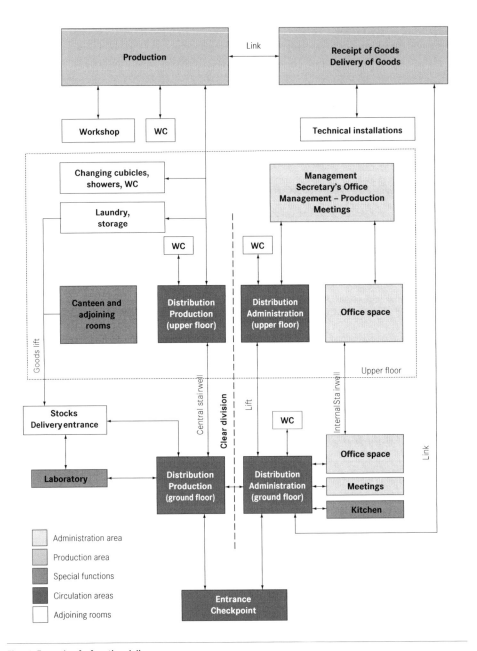

Fig. 41: Example of a functional diagram

It is important that you not equate the predefined spatial allocation plan with the actual architectural assignment and the purpose of the design. In fact, you should critically examine the plan and modify it if necessary. An architectural assignment transcends the pure function of a building. Moreover, the approaches described above should always be seen in relation to the other determinative factors.

For example, a community center will require not only a large hall with the affiliated secondary rooms and the necessary infrastructure. In order to fulfil its purpose, it must also be a place of encounter for diverse people and groups. So to design it successfully, you must grapple with soft factors in addition to the way processes and spaces function. These soft factors include accessibility, openness, lighting, atmosphere and views. These factors often cause conflict between the architectural assignment and the spatial allocation plan, which can be overcome by adapting the plan.

Constituents of design

When working with forms and design elements, you should always bear in mind that it is impossible to predict with any certainty the impact a design will have on others. A design is good not only because it satisfies the entire spectrum of individual requirements, but also – and more importantly – because the structure created defines the relationship of the individual elements to one another and thus arranges them in a new order. Exploring every possible solution by making sketches, drawings and models is the only way you can continually review your ideas and solutions.

The following chapter focuses on design as the initial point of departure in the design process. > Chapter Design basics

ORDER AND PROPORTION

Since Antiquity, proportions have been used to design facades and entire buildings. Their application can be seen in buildings throughout the ages: from the construction of temples in the ancient world to the building of medieval churches and Renaissance villas, and from the
■ architecture of classical Modernism to present-day structures.

Architects have repeatedly attempted to express ideal proportions with the aid of mathematical formulae. During classical Antiquity, they analyzed the proportions – especially in relation to dimensional ratios – of their temples and building elements (e.g. the different column orders). They then developed them further. Many Greek master builders and architects had a profound knowledge of geometry and used numerical ratios to arrange individual building elements in relation to one another when building temples.

■ **Tip:** The historical development of structural proportions is a fascinating subject. As you study this field, you will discover interesting parallels and developments, which have lost none of their relevance today. It is worth reading the books by Vitruvius, Alberti and Palladio, if you want to study the historical development of the laws of proportion in architecture (see Appendix, Literature).

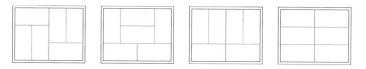

Fig. 42: Rooms made of six tatami mats

4:3	√2:1	3:2	Φ:1	5:3	16:9	2:1
=	=	=	=	=	=	=
1.3̄	1.414...	1.5	1.618...	1.6̄	1.7̄	2

Fig. 43: The customary proportions of rectangles

The double meaning of the concept of proportion is already contained in Vitruvius' definition (30 BC). On the one hand, the term "proportion" refers to the relationship of the parts to one another, and on the other, to human beings. For instance, the dimensions of the lower diameter of a Doric column in relation to its height form a ratio of 1:6, thus corresponding to the proportions of the male human body. The ratio of the height of an Ionic column to its diameter is 1:8, thus reflecting the proportions of a woman's body.

Japanese tatami mats provide a simple yet effective example of the application of proportional principles in architecture. Tatami mats are the basis upon which traditional Japanese houses are built. These mats generally measure 85 cm × 170 cm, although their dimensions may vary from region to region. Because of their 1:2 ratio, the mats can be arranged in an endless variety of constellations. The mats also determine both the size and proportions of rooms. (The standard Japanese room generally consists of six tatami mats.) > Fig. 42

Japanese tatami mats

In addition to the proportions of tatami mats, there are other proportions that are used in architecture and many other areas. > Fig. 43

One of the best-known proportions is the golden section, which expresses the relationship of two numbers or lengths in a ratio of approximately 1:1.618. The golden section is an irrational number, like the mathematical symbol π, because it cannot be expressed as a fraction of

The golden section

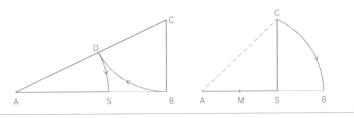

Fig. 44: Diagram showing how the golden section is derived

two whole numbers. Mathematically, the golden section is defined by the formula:

$$a/b = (a+b)/a$$

It can also be constructed with the aid of a circle. > Fig. 44

The Modulor   The introduction of the metric system ended the dominance of a wide variety of units of measure. Unlike the old units of length (inch, foot, yardstick and rod), the metre is related to the earth's circumference and not to human proportions. As a result, one of the two meanings of proportion – the direct relationship between the "modulus" and the human being – ceases to apply. Proceeding from a desire to reintroduce human scale into architecture, Le Corbusier developed his own system of measurement (the Modulor) from the proportions of the average human being and the golden section. The Modulor makes it possible to design proportions and dimensions that are directly related to their use, for example, in table and balustrade heights, as well as for the proportions of windows, entire rooms and
○ facades. > Fig. 45

Experiencing   Aside from all the mathematical approaches and analyses, propor-
proportions   tions create a subjective feeling of wellbeing in the viewer. Even though everyone can understand the desire for both systematization and directly

○ **Note:** If you want to learn more about the development of the Modulor and the background to the modular measuring system, see Le Corbusier: *The Modulor*, vols. 1 and 2, Birkhäuser, Basel 2000.

■ **Tip:** You can perform rewarding experiments using simple working models of cardboard, plasticine, wood and polystyrene blocks to create the forms and proportions you want. You will find further information on working models and modelmaking materials in *Basics Modelbuilding* by Alexander Schilling, Birkhäuser, Basel 2007.

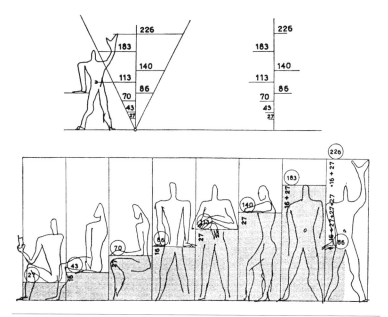

Fig. 45: Le Corbusier's Modulor

applicable rules, a great many seemingly well-designed buildings and facades are not based on any comprehensible mathematical rules. Thus, achieving balanced proportions always also means that designers must feel their way forwards when they determine the dimensions and compositions of various building elements and the relationships between them. ∎

For example, if you are working on the proportions of a facade, you will discover that there are a number of familiar rules and proportions you can fall back on. Even so, in many cases, facades only have well-designed proportions once you start to interpret and apply rules and proportions, or experiment until you arrive at the desired results. This may involve shifting and altering, say, a large panoramic window until you are satisfied with the proportions of the interior and the facade and they finally harmonize with the overall design.

BASIC ELEMENTS OF DESIGN

The geometry taught at school deals with points, straight lines, Geometrical forms planes, distances, angles etc. Working with the axioms established by Euclid (approx. 365–300 BC) and subsequent refinements of his theories, you can derive forms that will serve as a basis for your design. The two-dimensional forms (planes), for example, include the triangle, square,

rectangle, circle and rhombus; three-dimensional forms (bodies), on the other hand, include forms such as the cube, rectangular parallelepiped, sphere and cone. You can use these basic mathematical shapes to develop a variety of forms, ground plans and layouts by transforming
○ them, adding to them and subtracting sections from them.

Geometrical planes The geometrical properties of surfaces are largely transferred to the surface of the building. A square ground plan, which has four facades of equal length, is very suitable for designing what is basically a nondirectional building such as a pavilion in a park, or a building standing in an open space or a square. This applies even more to circular buildings, which are not only nondirectional, but also oriented to their own center, thus heightening the significance of space. Rectangular buildings, by contrast, have their own orientation. Their unidirectional alignment establishes front and side facades. Along the side facades, they form distinct three-dimensional edges, whereas the front facades create stop ends. An elliptical building, on the other hand, forms an aligned space with two focal points. Like a circular building, it also has one continuous facade. In contrast to the circle, however, the ellipse (not unlike a rectangular building) provides orientation. If you develop ground plans based on these geometrical figures, you should be able to recognize these laws and apply them consciously. The principles described here are shown in the examples in Figure 46.

Geometrical bodies By adding a third coordinate to the two-dimensional planes described above, you can create a variety of three-dimensional bodies. Geometrical bodies are subject to the same laws as surfaces.

Simple geometrical bodies are very striking and independent in character. They are especially suitable for designing object-like buildings set in spacious surroundings. > Figs. 47 and 48 Integrating such buildings into dense and heterogeneous settings where they stand close to other buildings is no easy task. The result is often a lack of clarity.

○ **Note:** Mathematics has played an important role in architecture ever since classical antiquity. Da Vinci's illustration of human proportions (1492) establishes a close relationship between the human body and geometrical forms. From time immemorial, architects have used basic geometrical forms to design ground plans, layouts, elevations and entire buildings.

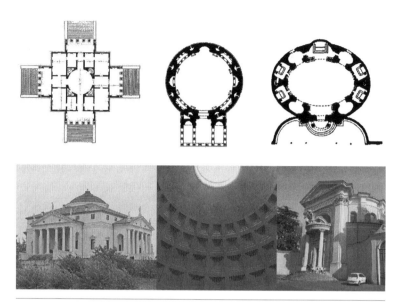

Fig. 46: Buildings with basic geometrical forms: La Rotonda, Pantheon, Sant Andrea di Quirinale

In addition to the material and immaterial relationships established by human beings, some forms and structures can be derived from nature, and they may give you ideas for your designs. Structures of this nature, which are often composed of organic shapes or forms derived from the environment, have captivating and richly varied contours. Most natural elements – even if they appear chaotic and randomly generated at first sight – are based on clear, albeit complex, patterns and rules. If you examine their cellular composition, you will discover structures that are unique with regard to their flexibility, loadbearing capacity, material efficiency and, above all, sculptural design. If you derive your ideas from nature, you will soon find inspiration in nature's formal language and diversity, too.

Forms found in nature

The Art Nouveau buildings of the late nineteenth and early twentieth centuries were an expression of their designers' interest in nature. The diverse styles within Art Nouveau reveal a variety of ways in which architects were inspired by nature: from floral ornamentation to flowing, lively ground plans and facades to the organic design of entire buildings. > Fig. 49

Art Nouveau

Fig. 47: Right-angled cubes look compact in their surroundings

Fig. 48: Examples of the use of geometrical forms, cylinders and pyramids

Fig. 49: Art Nouveau forms inspired by nature

○ **Note:** The term "bionics" is composed of the first syllable of the word biology and the second syllable of the word technics. Bionics endeavors to apply the method, structural and development principles of nature to technical systems.

Furthermore, studying nature can be very helpful if you wish to transform organizational and structural principles into constructed architecture.

○

Many architects have developed or refined their building designs and structures by applying bionic principles. The tent-like cablenet structure designed by Frei Otto at the Olympic Park in Munich, the "bubble-and-foam" geodesic domes in Grimshaw's Eden Project, and Calatrava's bridges and buildings (whose ribs and loadbearing structures look like skeletons), have all been developed from structural principles that exist in nature. If you want to transform nature into technology, you will have to work your way through continuous processes of modification and abstraction, because natural forms are far too complex to be faithfully copied. Observing and analysing the principles upon which natural forms are based is far more important, for only then can the insights gained be transformed into architectural structures. Frei Otto developed roof forms by experimenting with steel cables and soap bubbles. The forms he created are produced by gravitational force alone and ideally reproduce the flows of force in the roof skin. > Figs. 50, 51, and Chapter Working with materials and structures, Materials and structures as design elements

Bionics

Plants and animals display a wide variety of features that can be adapted and transferred to buildings. Examples include the skeleton of a living creature, the compound eye of an insect, the shell of an armadillo and the wings of a bird. > Figs. 52-55

If you try to arrive at a design form by experimenting with structures and constructions, you will be able to create forms that, at first sight, may seem to have nothing to do with order-creating systems and are fascinating for their sheer novelty. In its endeavour to create freely flowing forms, architecture comes very close to the other fine arts. This approach is particularly suitable for the design of large-scale building projects of social significance: churches, museums, cultural centers etc. Frequently, the goal of the design process is to make a building more dynamic and to render movement inside and around a building visible. Such strategies have been used in designing leaning structures with rounded-off edges or structures whose forms only become apparent during museum visits, or forms that spiral continuously through the building. > Figs. 56 and Chapters Constituents of design, Space and bodies and Arriving at ideas

Free forms

Free forms are particularly useful for giving a building a symbolic character or lending a space or a building a unique appearance. The danger with this approach, however, is that it can lead architects to devote too much attention to the form and too little to the other demands placed on the building. > Fig. 57

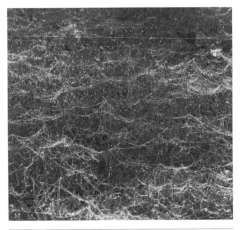

Fig. 50: Baldachin spider's web on a meadow

Fig. 51: A roof made of a cablenet structure

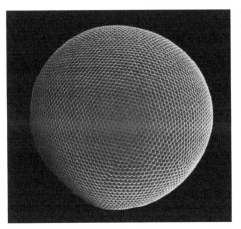

Fig. 52: The compound eye of the Antarctic crill

Fig. 53: The Eden Project in Cornwall

Fig. 54: A mute swan spreading its wings

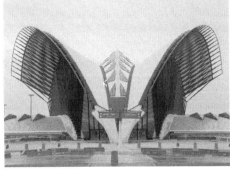

Fig. 55: TGV railway station in Lyon

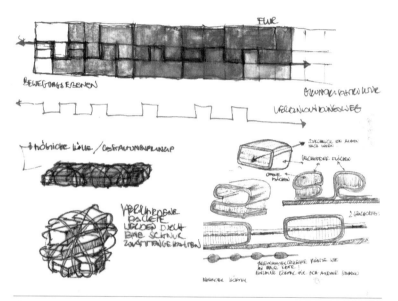

Fig. 56: Dynamic free forms in modernist architecture

Fig. 57: Sketches made in the search for forms

SPACE AND BODIES

Architecture is always the result of interactions between spaces and bodies. Each body defines spaces; objects only become legible in space. These elements are opposites. They are also mutually and directly dependent on one another. Only in their interaction do space and body form a whole. And architecture is possible only as a result of their interaction. Flowing successions of rooms often exist between clearly defined spaces and disbodies, with room sequences, gaps, and exterior and interior rooms emerging from the fertile interplay of both elements.

Body with joint   Adjoining bodies   Penetration

Fig. 58: Various principles for adding two bodies

If you want your design to consist of more than just a basic form, you will find there are various ways of using a number of different of elements. You can create space by arranging and joining several elements. You can subtract bodies to create space or to modify and transform basic ele-
■ ments. There are endless ways of combining these methods.

Arranging and joining elements

If you want to create complex figures by means of addition, you must position the elements in your design in relationship to one another. You can choose a number of different solitary forms that interact through their form alone, or identical bodies that enter into a relationship through the way you arrange them.

Forms can interpenetrate or cut into one another, attach or be added to other forms, form rows or fit into one another. They always interact and create spatial structures. > Figs. 58 and 59 You have two basic choices here: you can either create space between two elements by arranging them in a certain way, or you can arrange the elements in a given space. > Fig. 60

■ **Tip:** The book *Architecture – Form, Space and Order* by Francis D. K. Ching is a standard work that explains the basic relationships between bodies and space (see Appendix, Literature).

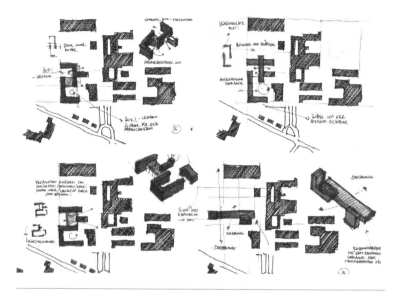

Fig. 59: Sketches illustrating the addition of bodies to an urban context

In addition to arranging two or three forms to create a composition, you will discover that there are situations (e.g. in urban and settlement development) in which a far greater number of forms must be coherently arranged. Typical arrangements include > Fig. 61

— Rows
— Grids
— Clusters or groups
— The arrangement of buildings round squares or other central points
— Radial arrangements
— Elements strung out like a pearl necklace

The slab is a very special form of structure. It can be arranged horizontally or vertically. It can also be used to create paths and to steer people toward certain destinations. Depending on whether slabs are aligned to create a path or make a visual impact, they can be used to create spaces that flow into one another or interlock internal and external spaces. > Fig. 62

Creating space with slabs

You should take into account not only the arrangement of the slabs on the ground plan, but also the impression created by the profile of the horizontal slabs, because it decisively influences the impact of the

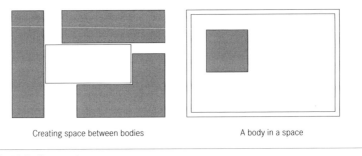

Creating space between bodies   A body in a space

Fig. 60: Bodies creating space

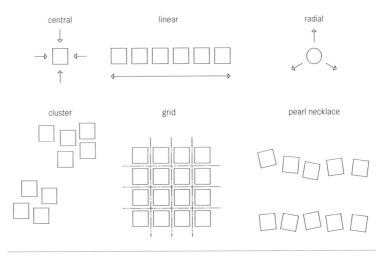

central   linear   radial

cluster   grid   pearl necklace

Fig. 61: Ways of arranging buildings

design. The vertical position of the base plate can play a vital role in determining a building's impact. It can be: > Figs. 63 and 64

— Sunk into its foundations
— Flush
— Lying directly at ground level
— Floating above it

Subtraction and modification You can develop surfaces and bodies by modifying or subtracting sections from them. For example, a fragmentary body can serve as the geometric basis for a design. Simple basic forms such as squares and circles can be varied and modified in countless ways. > Figs. 65–67

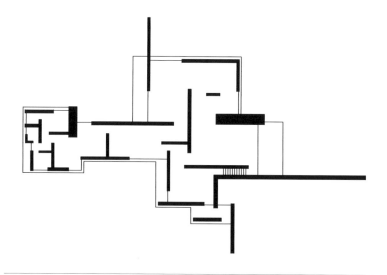

Fig. 62: Flowing spaces (copy of a design by Mies van der Rohe)

Fig. 63: Horizontal slabs arranged parallel to the terrain

Fig. 64: Examples of well-known Modernist slab houses

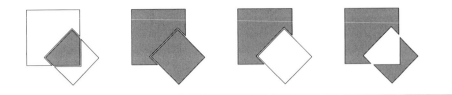

Fig. 65: Variations from set theory

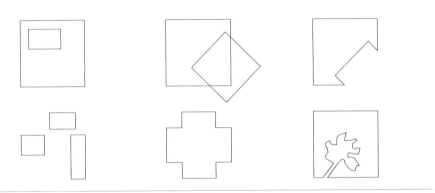

Fig. 66: Subtractive and modified squares

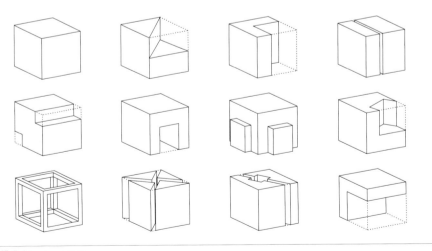

Fig. 67: Subtractive cubes

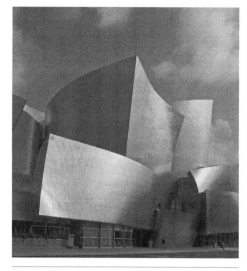

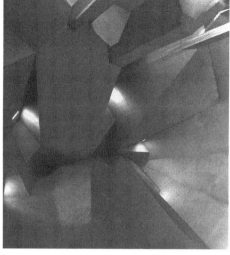

Fig. 68: Bent bodies and surfaces **Fig. 69: Folding as a design principle**

Many of these variations are based on simple mathematical functions taken from set theory. If two bodies or surfaces intersect, they open up a number of possibilities, creating subsets, intersections, unions and differences.

Another way of modifying or transforming bodies and surfaces is to fold or bend them. By bending or folding a strip, you can create a channelled spatial flow that contains and redirects space. By turning or bending a body, you can counteract its geometric rigidity, thereby making it softer and more ductile. Alternatively, you can change the basic form to take into account external influences and forces, which become apparent only when the form is transformed or deformed. > Figs. 68 and 69 In addition to transforming geometric elements by folding and bending them, you can also create and process far more complex forms, and freely create new designs using a computer.

Folding and bending

Working with materials and structures

Historically, the starting point of design was the structure, which again came into its own at the dawn of the industrial age. In general, the architect will ensure that the structure, which is the building's basic frame, is visible in the final product. In skeleton structures, the structure may assume the form of a column grid that defines the facade system and the interior. Since the industrial revolution, engineered structures, such as bridges, have openly displayed their structural design, giving them a legible loadbearing structure. This development led at the end of the nineteenth century to the emergence of a new aesthetic that rejected the practice of cladding and decorating structures. Evidence of this can be seen in many areas of architecture too. In such cases, there is a direct and close relationship between the structure and materials used. Without the industrial production of iron, for example, filigree industrial buildings would be inconceivable. And without the properties of reinforced concrete, most shell structures could never have been constructed in their present form. > Fig. 70 A material's technical, visual and tactile properties can be consciously used to add expression to a design and the ensuing structure.

MATERIALS AND STRUCTURES AS DESIGN ELEMENTS

The structure can be exploited to shape and structure the design. Alternatively, you can develop your design from the context or the function, or by creating your own forms and then integrating the required structure later on in a way that renders it imperceptible. In the case of buildings with demanding structural requirements (e.g. wide spans), it is very difficult to treat the function, form and structure separately. Hence, it may be advisable to take the loadbearing structure as the starting point of both the design process and all further developments.

Fig. 70: A reinforced concrete hyperbolic paraboloid

If you want to use the structure as the basis for your design, you will have to familiarize yourself with the technical criteria for constructing loadbearing structures, i.e. the static systems, the choice of materials and the dimensions of the elements.

Generally speaking, the material from which a building is to be con- Structure and choice of materials structed is chosen during the design process. The material can, however, serve as the basis of the design. Natural stone may lend the surroundings their particular character, or the surrounding structures may be wooden buildings that were chosen for climatic reasons. > Chapter Designing in context, Social and socio-cultural factors The choice of material may be inspired by the original idea for the structure you wish to build. If your design is based on a specific material, you will have to take the properties of the material into account when you develop your structure or design. > Fig. 71 ○

In general, the structure not only establishes order and supports The structure as a design element loads, but in many cases also serves as the central feature of the design. The design ought to enhance both the loadbearing capacity of the structure and the use of the material. It can also decisively influence both the aesthetic appearance and the structure of a work of architecture.

Once you know the requirements and the static conditions, you can get down to the truly creative part of the work. There are many different ways of using loadbearing structures creatively. For example, distances can be spanned by linear girders, a loadbearing grid, flat building elements, cable supports or curved shells. Each of these loadbearing systems can determine the choice of design and the structure's spatial impact. Even if spatial considerations demand specific structural loadbearing systems, you can still purposefully use these systems to develop forms and structures that transcend their basic function as supports. You can also design different types of connections such as hinged supports and erection joints intended for use with specific materials.

○ **Note:** Further tips on the choice of material and structure can be found in the following volumes in the "Basics" series:

Basics Materials by Manfred Hegger, Hans Drexler and Martin Zeumer

Basics Loadbearing Systems by Alfred Meistermann
Basics Timber Construction by Ludwig Steiger
Basics Masonry Construction by Nils Kummer
Basics Glass Construction by Andreas Achilles and Diane Navratil

Fig. 71: Individual structures made of plastic, masonry, concrete and wood, which embody the specific properties of the materials

Fig. 72: Loadbearing structures that make excellent use of the materials from which they are made

You need a sound knowledge of statics if you want to develop interesting structures that do not rely on standardized elements. The important thing here, however, is not whether you are able to calculate loadbearing structures precisely, but whether you have a good grasp of structures and static systems. You can also develop innovative ideas by experimenting with gravity. In doing so, you can develop internally stable static systems with the aid of small models, and save having to per-
■ form extensive calculations.

■ **Tip:** The Spanish architect Santiago Calatrava has made many static models that serve as the basis for his often daring buildings. If you are interested in developing designs of this nature, you may find Calatrava's static experiments a good source of inspiration in developing your own ideas.

You can obtain parameters for designs und forms by examining the structural rules and material properties of certain building materials. Masonry, for example, is of limited use for bridging wide gaps and is therefore often used in vaulted or arched structures. On the other hand, if you are constructing wooden buildings, you must consider the alignment of the material and take structural measures to protect the wood. Steel structures permit large spans with a minimal use of material, although their fire protection behaviour is problematic. No matter what material you choose, the structure should take into account its specific properties so that you exploit them to the full. > Fig. 72

A structure that does justice to the material

Once you have chosen your material, its potential and the functional requirements will generally dictate the span lengths and the distances between the different structural elements in your design. A grid is created by repeating measured areas (if this is desired and forms the basis of the design). Modular grids are used in the development of organizational systems, facades and spaces.

Modular grids and span lengths

Grids can consist of axes set at right angles to each other to form rectangular or quadratic fields. As an alternative, you might consider using grids with arbitrary angles and rhomboid fields, or triangular grids with equilateral triangles. The grid used in a linear loadbearing structure is based on linear spaces without a second directional axis. > Fig. 73

In this connection, the question usually arises as to whether the facades and non-bearing walls should rest on the grid axes or be offset against them. If the structure combines a skeleton and a solid structure in which the walls and the supports both assume loadbearing functions, it may be advisable to place the walls on the grid axes, thus breaking down the walls into rows of columns. By offsetting the walls and facade – as in a pure skeleton structure – against the grid, you will create a clear distinction between the loadbearing and the space-bordering elements. The structure, which will include some freestanding columns, will have far greater presence and appear more autonomous. > Fig. 74

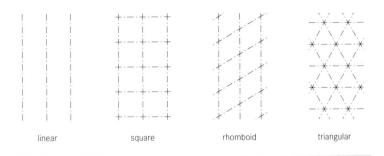

| linear | square | rhomboid | triangular |

Fig. 73: Types of grids

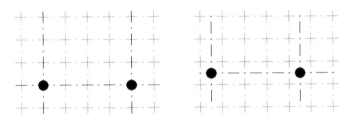

Fig. 74: Integrated and freestanding columns

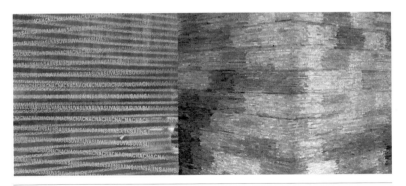

Fig. 75: Examples of the different effects of glass: interference by layering broken glass and imprinting

HOW WE PERCEIVE MATERIALS

Materials are distinguished not only by their technical properties, but also by their effect on the viewer. We perceive materials in different ways through the interplay of our various sense organs.

Fig. 76: Dematerialized floating glass bodies

Fig. 77: The old and the new in the contrast between stone and light structures

As almost 90 percent of all stimuli are perceived visually, the visual impact of buildings and materials has played an important role throughout the history of architecture, and has often been the object of study. Sensory perception

It is quite difficult to capture and represent the sound, smell and tactile qualities of a building with the standard methods and tools of design. Such perceptions can be derived from their function or context only to a limited degree, because they are intimately connected to the material properties of a building. > Fig. 75 Materials and the atmosphere

The skilful and correct use of materials can buttress your design statement or even be the very thing that makes it work. Attributes that are important in this context include:

— Stony, earthy
— Light, floating
— Concealing
— Layered
— Transparent, translucent
— Open, closed

With glass, you can more or less dematerialize a light body. Using earthy materials, on the other hand, you can enhance the structure of subtractive forms. If you use flexible, transparent building materials, you can create the impression that the shell is detaching itself from a building. > Figs. 76 and 77

Arriving at ideas

There are as many ways of arriving at an idea for a design as there are of practising architecture in general. The design process often starts unconsciously, or it may be inspired by an experience or an event that awakens your interest and stimulates your imagination. Such "events" are generally the various kinds of external impulses described above. They influence the architect creating the design or form the bases of experiences that he or she can draw on. Once you have developed your first ideas, you need to consider how you want to execute them and explore the potential of the different approaches.

Remaining true to an ideal

When working on a design, you will often discover that you cannot adhere strictly to your first idea from start to finish. Diverse parameters and basic ideas will necessitate a variety of options and design approaches. You may find inspiring ideas in different approaches and wish to pursue these further. There is, of course, the danger that you will water down good principles by combining them with others or by being too hesitant. You should keep your original principle in mind at all times, even if it means sacrificing other ideas. Abandoning a good idea in favor of another one is not always a disadvantage, because succinctness and legibility may enhance the quality of your design. When you start working on new projects, you may find yourself returning to ideas you had abandoned earlier. In this way, your ideas will broaden your knowledge.

Simple but not banal

Remaining true to an idea and searching for simple concepts also entails the risk of becoming banal or one-dimensional and sacrificing the complexity and subtlety of a design for the sake of clarity. Designs and buildings – just like the demands placed on a building – should be multidimensional and varied. However, variety also calls for complete clarity in the formulation of details. Many interesting designs are based on a clear principle that is faithfully executed down to the last detail. That said, your basic idea should not become a dogma. Nor should it mean reducing everything to this one principle. Make sure that the defining elements in your design articulate the design statement and do not detract from it. And do not forget that different principles can be allowed to overlap in different parts of the design so that they mutually supplement and enhance one another.

Tools and techniques of presentation

The presentation technique and tools you choose can greatly influence the design process. As in crafting an object, the result of your work depends on these tools.

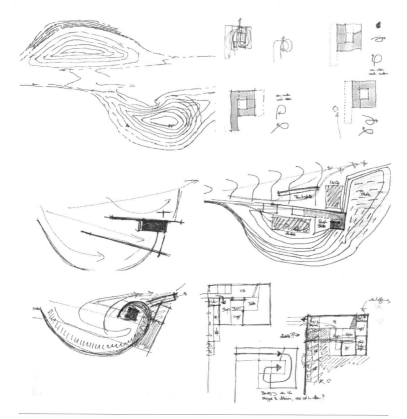

Fig. 78: Preliminary design ideas drawn with pencil and paper

Pencils are very good for developing plans, sketching the ground plan, the framework, and the contours. > Fig. 78 The ground plan provides an ideal basis for studying and developing spatial structures and horizontal movements, as well as for organizing and zoning a design. It also allows you to represent vertical relations and spatial proportions in system sections. The facades provide a good starting point for developing and designing the room lighting, the building's interaction with the exterior and the outward appearance of the building. On the other hand, if you use media and presentation techniques that are both novel and unfamiliar, you may come up with some new and innovative solutions. > Chapter Arriving at ideas, Methods and strategies Over the past ten years, computer-aided design has made it possible to create building forms that would have been difficult to visualize with analogue tools such as pencils. One particular new trend – itself a product of the manifold possibilities of the digital world –

Fig. 79: Computer-generated forms (blobs)

is called blob architecture, which uses free-form curves (splines) with complex, flowing and often rounded and biomorphic shapes. Only the use of modern design and visualization software has made such designs

■ ○ possible. > Fig. 79

Architectural students are recommended to try out various approaches so that they can find out which "manual" aids are best suited to intuitive approaches, and which ones best support and stimulate their creativity.

CREATIVITY AND CREATIVITY TECHNIQUES

When students first begin studying, they often wonder whether they will be able to fulfil the demands their college makes on their creativity as designers. They try to judge their own creativity and their design abil-

■ **Tip:** Despite the potential of CAD programs, many architects find it difficult to design buildings with them because they cannot be used intuitively (in contrast to pencils and other tools). New students experience these programs in much the same way. For this reason, it is advisable to work with CAD software only if the manual side of design (e.g. working with a pencil) no longer absorbs a lot of your attention or if you have access to programs that allow you to design volumes and objects intuitively.

○ **Note:** If you are interested in background information on blobs and their development, we recommend the articles by Jeffrey Kipnis "Towards a New Architecture" and Greg Lyn "Architectural Curvilinearity: The Folded, the Pliant and the Supple" (both in *Theories and Manifestoes of Contemporary Architecture,* 2nd edition).

ities on the basis of their previous experience, which they tend to project onto the architectural course. To what extent is originality necessary for an architectural design? What role does creativity play in the design process?

When studying a design, you will rarely find yourself standing before a white canvas on which you can "paint" anything you like. There are certain parameters that influence a design process and often determine its points of departure and the directions it will take. During the design process, you will rarely develop ideas that have never existed before. The main challenge lies in developing new solutions based on existing principles and design approaches. Consequently, regardless of a person's individual potential, creativity should always be stimulated by external influences, the things that a person has already learned and the will to develop them further.

Creativity

○

Science has developed a variety of creative techniques that are very useful in architectural design. These techniques aim to produce a large number of ideas intuitively in a short period of time. They trigger associations and new ways of thinking about problems. They also aim to activate hidden ideas and minimize inhibitions. Interaction between group participants is a very stimulating way of finding new solutions.

In brainstorming sessions, a group is established and assigned a specific task. First, the task is explained and analyzed. If required, a typical solution is presented. Then all the members are invited to submit spontaneous suggestions and ideas without criticizing one another or making judgmental statements about the others' ideas. Only in this way are group members discouraged from thinking through all the consequences of an idea first and encouraged to feel at liberty to express themselves freely. Even absurd ideas can motivate one member to come up with an alternative approach and thus encourage others to stimulate one another. All the proposals are noted down during the course of the session and then, when it draws to a close, presented and evaluated in terms of their feasibility.

Brainstorming

○ **Note:** People generally associate the term creativity with a solution that solves a problem or a task in a novel, effective and, in most cases, unconventional way. It is quite possible that without creativity a specific problem would never be identified or solved. Furthermore, it helps you to approach a problem flexibly and with new resources that were previously unavailable in a specific context.

Brainwriting

Brainwriting follows the same procedure as brainstorming, the difference being that the ideas are not submitted to the group, but written down by each member. This makes it easier for the more reserved members to present their ideas.

Gallery method

A technique often used to encourage creativity, especially in architectural courses, is called the gallery method. Each of the participants writes down his or her solution, which is then shown with the other solutions on a display surface. The solutions are discussed during an association phase (colloquium) and then refined on the basis of the new insights that have arisen. Afterward the revised solutions are presented for criticism by the other group members.

SCAMPER

SCAMPER is a creative technique that functions like a checklist. It aims to discover new directions and to question prevailing ideas. > Tab. 2 By answering questions about specific points, participants can try to find variations on designs and ways out of possible dead-ends.

Tab. 2: SCAMPER-Method

Abbreviation	Meaning	
S	Substitute	Replace individual elements
C	Combine	Combine with other elements or combine different elements with one another
A	Adapt	Adapt content or functions
M	Modify	Modify the size or the scale; vary elements
P	Put	Put to other uses
E	Eliminate	Eliminate added elements, reduce to core function
R	Reserve	Turn upside down, diametrically opposed ideas

Mind maps

A mind map is a diagram presenting a task. The central task is written on the center of a page and visually linked with subordinate aspects and variations. If, for example, you are trying to study a design assignment and its function, a mind map may help you to develop functional schemes. > Fig. 80 and Chapter Design and function, Spatial allocation plan and internal organization

Working methods for lone designers

Even if you do not work in a group and are searching for a design idea on your own, you might still find the above-mentioned creativity techniques useful. To avoid the danger of becoming creatively blocked during the design process, it is a good idea to examine and question both yourself and your design as it take shape, and to consider these different aspects in a different light and from a different angle (e.g. that of an

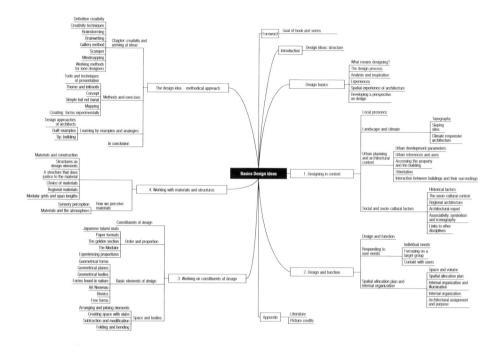

Fig. 80: A mind map for the book *Basics Design Ideas*

outsider). Discussions with others – including people working in other fields – can be helpful. You can also place yourself in the position of subsequent users and try to see the design through their eyes so that you can study a building's impact on them.

It is often advisable to take regular breaks and occupy yourself with other things for a while in order to put some distance between yourself and your design idea or the particular line of thought you are pursuing. This will allow you to challenge and critically evaluate the principles underlying your design through the eyes of an outsider.

METHODS AND STRATEGIES

Usually, one of the very first tasks you face involves examining the above-mentioned design parameters. There is no way of knowing which approaches will be successful. It may be best to visit the site. While you are making sketches, taking photographs and studying the wider surroundings, you will develop you first ideas for your design. Analysing the spatial and urban context in order to get a feel for an area is often a worthwhile endeavor. This is particularly important if you are dealing with an area unfamiliar to you.

Analyses and surveys

Models and
built examples Another method is to study other buildings designed to solve similar tasks or conceived in a similar context, so that you can get a feel for the assignment. If the planning assignment involves a special function (such as a railway station, or a building site located on a slope) that makes it difficult to survey the surroundings, examining examples of constructed buildings can give you useful clues on how to solve the problem. The more you study examples of constructed buildings, the greater the range of variations and choices available to you will be. When developing your design, you should remember that aesthetic sensibilities are not the only criteria that count. You should also take into account the general conditions, try to visualize and analyze a building or vision in its specific context and develop your own ideas and approach accordingly. > Chapter Designing in context

Design approaches of
famous architects Another method is to study the works of a well-known architect and to try to develop a design by applying his or her guiding principles and ideas. While you are designing your project, you will gain a much deeper understanding of the architect's work and standpoint. By applying the contents to one of your own designs, you will be able to relate to it and develop your own approach as you see fit.

Theme and leitmotif Frequently, buildings do not embody an identifiable design idea. This is often due to the great number of functions buildings are supposed to perform and to the fact that these functions often have to be given more or less equal treatment during the design phase. To ensure that your design has an identity, you might assign it a theme or leitmotif, or find a good foundation. Sometimes, leitmotifs can be found outside the normal context of architectural design.

You may find inspiration for themes from both the material objects and immaterial phenomena that you transform into elements of your design. The difficulty lies in correctly defining the degree of abstraction that this transformation entails. If you select a theme that is distinguished by very explicit motifs and associations, make sure that your design does not appear simplistic or banal because you have directly adopted the motif in your design. At the same time, you should also ensure that your motif does not lose all relevance to the original theme by appearing overly abstract. Your design should respond subtly to thematic influences. > Figs. 81–83 These exercises will help you learn how to use referential motifs, abstractions and symbolic elements.

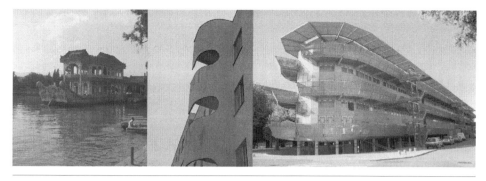

Fig. 81: Realizations of the "ship" leitmotif in different epochs

Fig. 82: The "evolution" leitmotif, interpreted as a spiral that museum visitors walk through parallel to the thematic exhibits

Fig. 83: The "island" leitmotif for the design of a housing estate in the forest

Mapping is a special form of transcription and a particular way of developing a design theme. It allows you to develop an architectural structure that relates to spatial phenomena at the future construction site and serves as a basis for your design. The actual process of mapping can involve taking photographs and videos or making sketches and models. The data are then evaluated using a specially developed logic and a language – a special system of notation – that concentrates on spatial phenomena (e.g. spaces for movement, light and shadow, gaps, noises etc.). The

Mapping

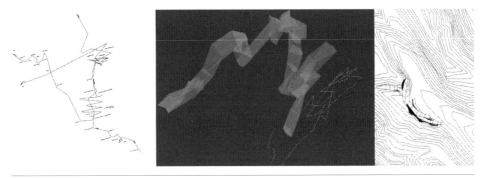

Fig. 84: From mapping to design

notation is designed to translate spatial phenomena into a model architectural structure. > Fig. 84 This highly intense and undoubtedly subjective
analysis of the property will allow you to study the site closely and pre-
○ pare yourself more effectively for the task at hand.

Creating forms   Instead of approaching the task analytically, you can also arrive at
experimentally   an initial thematic position by creating forms experimentally. You can perform this task on a computer using design and visualization software or
by using analogue, sculptural models (e.g. gypsum, wax, plasticine). You
can digitize your results later using a three-dimensional scanner or other
equipment. By experimenting with traditional materials from different
contexts, you can create unanticipated, innovative forms.

○ **Note:** The term "mapping" is derived from the word
map. Maps deal with facts. They are graphic represen-
tations of dimensions, attributes and relationships
between elements in the physical world or in the world
of logic. Almost everything can be illustrated or
recorded: spaces, galaxies, time, history, occupations
and philosophies. If you are interested in this subject,
we recommend *Mapping* by Roger Fawcett-Tang and
William Owe, RotoVision, 2005.

Fig. 85: Constructed examples based on forms created experimentally

The many available methods include:

— Deriving a form from crumpled-up paper (Frank O. Gehry does this
 when he is preparing his studies)
— Deforming an object (e.g. a can or a cardboard box) to create
 complex geometric forms
— Creating structures using magnetism: e.g. arranging iron filings
 or nails on a table
— Processing plasticine on a board to create dynamic forms

Experimental work may initially seem to have an accidental or ran-
dom quality, but this is only true to a certain extent. You will generally
find yourself experimenting with ideas and discarding results until you
know you have finally got a structure with potential. You can then set
about refining and optimizing it. In this way, the experiment serves as a
catalyst for your creativity. The next stages of the design process pro-
ceed – as with basic geometric forms – from this first move. The exciting thing is that, whatever approach you choose, you can identify the
functional and aesthetic potential in the forms you have created. > Fig. 85 ■

■ **Tip:** Many new currents and approaches have come
about over the past few years through people putting
everyday objects and materials to uses other than
those intended and developing them further by modifying them to create specific forms and loadbearing
systems. Seeking such potential with open eyes is an
exciting way of transgressing the boundaries of con-
ventional formal language.

In conclusion

Although the quality of an architectural design is manifested in certain characteristic features such as the consistency of the concept and the differentiated approach to the site, judgements on quality always include subjective perception. Architectural quality cannot really be judged in terms of objective parameters or scales. An evaluation always includes the subjective views of the evaluator. Periodic changes in taste beyond the lifetime of a building also play a role. Buildings that were modern in the 1980s may now appear outdated, whilst late nineteenth-century Central European (*Gründerzeit*) buildings overladen with stucco are currently very popular, despite the derision poured on them by the Modernists for being kitschy. Regardless of whether a design is made to be "timeless" or whether it directly reflects contemporary tastes, it will only be truly consistent if it is well conceived and executed without any loss in quality. The design process evolves out of an initial idea; the design gradually takes shape. The aim now is to transfer the principles and the basic idea underlying the design into the plans; to work out the details; and to steer the project through to the construction stage.

The present book is intended to be a source of inspiration for designers – in full awareness of the fact that it merely goes through the preliminary phase of a process. The methods presented indicate various – and by no means definitive – ways of tackling design assignments. Design does not involve simply reproducing certain processes or existing models. It is always a creative process that produces new totalities under a variety of conditions and draws on diverse sources of inspiration. The elements that we have examined independently in this book to come up with our first design ideas – context, function, design, material and structure – must interact closely throughout the design process to create a complex system of influences and conditions. Which of these elements gives birth to the first design idea and which approach leads to a mature concept? The answer lies in individual experience and insights. What is more, a course in architecture provides an invaluable basis for gaining them. Design is not something you can learn passively from books or lectures, which merely provide stimuli or act as catalysts for students' individual development. Design is something you learn by doing – through practical experience. I hope that the book *Design Ideas* provides useful stimuli for making your own creative designs and encourages you to devote yourself to every aspect of design. Above all, I hope that it will help you, in the long term, to find your own path in design. This means that you must never stop asking questions, and that you will always be willing to experiment, that you retain your curiosity and find pleasure in working on your own designs.

Appendix

LITERATURE

Design basics

Leon Battista Alberti: *The ten Books of Architecture: the 1755 Leoni Edition,* New York 1986

Francis D. K. Ching: *Architecture. Form, Space and Order,* 3rd edition, John Wiley & Sons, New York 2007

Le Corbusier: *The Modulor, Modulor 2,* Birkhäuser, Basel 2000

Roger Fawcett-Tang, William Owen: *Mapping,* RotoVision, Brighton 2005

Christian Gänshirt: *Werkzeuge für Ideen,* Birkhäuser, Basel 2011

Jeffrey Kipnis: *InFormation/DeFormation,* in *Arch+,* No. 131

Greg Lynn: *Das Gefaltete, das Biegsame und das Geschmeidige,* in *Arch+,* No. 131

Andrea Palladio: *The four Books on Architecture,* MIT Press, Cambridge/MA 1997

Camillo Sitte: *City Planning according to artistic Principles,* Phaidon, Berlin 1965

Vitruvius: *Ten Books on Architecture,* Cambridge University Press, Cambridge 2002

Architectural history and theory

Otl Aicher: *The World as Design,* 2nd edition, Ernst, Berlin 2015

Leonardo Benevolo: *The European City,* Blackwell, Oxford 1993

Le Corbusier: *Towards a new Architecture,* Dover Publications, London 1986

Siegfried Giedion: *Space, Time and Architecture: The Growth of a new Tradition,* Harvard University Press, Cambridge/MA 2003

Hanno-Walter Kruft: *A History of architectural Theory from Vitruvius to the Present,* Zwemmer, London 1994

Robert Venturi: *Complexity and Contradiction in Architecture,* Little Brown & Co, Boston 1977

Robert Venturi, Denise Scott Brown, Steven Izenour: *Learning from Las Vegas,* MIT Press, Boston 1972

Different focuses on design

Jürgen Adam, Katharina Hausmann, Frank Jüttner: *Entwurfsatlas Industriebau,* Birkhäuser, Basel 2004

Sophia und Stefan Behling: *Solar Power,* Prestel Publishing, Munich 2000

Mark Dudek: *Entwurfsatlas Schulen und Kindergärten,* 2nd edition, Birkhäuser, Basel 2011

Roberto Gonzalo, Karl J. Habermann: *Energy-Efficient Architecture,*
    Birkhäuser, Basel 2006
Rainer Hascher, Simone Jeska, Birgit Klauck: *Office Buildings.*
    A Design Manual, Birkhäuser, Basel 2002
Paul von Naredi-Rainer: *Entwurfsatlas Museumsbau*, Birkhäuser, Basel
    2004
Ernst Neufert: *Architect's Data,* Wiley-Blackwell, Chichester 2012
Friedericke Schneider (ed.): *Floor Plan Manual. Housing,* Birkhäuser,
    Basel 2011

PICTURE CREDITS

THE AUTHORS

Bert Bielefeld, Prof. Dr.-Ing. Architect, Professor for construction
    economics and construction management at the University
    of Siegen, executive partner of bertbielefeld&partner architekten
    ingenieure
Sebastian El Khouli, Dipl.-Ing. Arch. (TU), energy consultant
    (TU Darmstadt), senior staff member Bob Gysin + Partner BGP
    Architekten Zurich

Series editor: Bert Bielefeld
Concept: Bert Bielefeld, Annette Gref
Translation from German into English:
Michael Robinson
English copy editing: Monica Buckland
Project management: Annette Gref
Layout, cover design, and typography:
Andreas Hidber
Production and typesetting: Amelie Solbrig

Papier: MultiOffset, 120 g/m²
Druck: Beltz Grafische Betriebe GmbH

Library of Congress Control Number:
2019938300

Bibliographic information published by the
German National Library
The German National Library lists this publica-
tion in the Deutsche Nationalbibliografie;
detailed bibliographic data are available on the
Internet at http://dnb.dnb.de.

This book is also available as an e-book
(ISBN PDF 978-3-0356-1237-0; ISBN EPUB
978-3-0356-1135-9) and in a German language
edition (ISBN Print 978-3-0346-0675-2).

© 2019 Birkhäuser Verlag GmbH, Basel
P.O. Box 44, 4009 Basel, Switzerland
Part of Walter de Gruyter GmbH, Berlin/Boston

ISBN 978-3-0356-1745-0

9 8 7 6 5 4 3 2

www.birkhauser.com